NORWAY'S COASTAL VOYAGE

PÅL ESPOLIN JOHNSON

TRANSLATED BY DONNA LUNNEY VEAR AND IAN WATERING

TO THE

NORWAY'S COASTAL VOYAGE
TOP OF THE WORLD

CAPPELEN

Endpaper:
A Mai morning near the
Arctic Circle.

View from a southbound
vessel sailing through Vesterålen
on a summer day.

© J.W.Cappelens Forlag A/S
Grøndahl Dreyer, 2000
Produced by: Boksenteret Erik
Pettersen & Co. A/S

Photos: Unless otherwise noted,
photos have been taken by the author.
Photo on cover:
Vivi Brit Espolin Johnson
Map: Geir Tandberg Steigan

Cover and design: Kai Øvre
Prepress: PDC Tangen / Capella Media
Printed by: Eurolitho 2000
5th printing, 2000

ISBN 82-02-19607-8

CONTENTS

A STRING OF PEARLS

An elderly gentleman, his dog on a leash, pauses on his evening stroll and looks at his watch, and smiles contentedly: "There she is, on time as always!" He waits for a moment watching the beautiful ship and dreaming that he is on board, until an impatient tug at the leash reminds him that it is time to move on. Night is approaching in Bergen. The northbound coastal steamer has cast off and is heading out along the calm waters of Salhusfjord east of Askøya.

In the reception onboard the purser is sitting in the glow of the computer screen checking the passenger list. In the noise and heat of the engine room the ship's engineer is pottering about with an oil-can and soiled rag, whilst up in the mess the cook and the deck man share a pot of coffee. In the half-light up on the bridge the captain and mate converse quietly, while keeping a watchful eye on the beacons, the navigation channel and the instrument panel.

This evening, like every other evening, a piece of Norway has left port. Men, women, novices and old hands. A whole little community on its way northwards.

Every evening of the year a coastal steamer sets out from the port of Bergen on the 2500 nautical mile voyage to Kirkenes and back. At the same moment that M/S "Nordnorge" or M/S "Polarlys" is pulling away from the quayside in Bergen, another coastal steamer is ply-

A new landfall – heaving line at the ready. Most of the crew were born and bred along the coast and have seen coastal steamers come and go since they played on the quayside.

■

ing the waves across the inhospitable Hustadvika bound for Kristiansund (famous for its klipfish). A third is pushing along the coast of Trøndelag on its way towards the thousands of skerries and islands of Helgeland. A fourth is sailing past the jagged peaks of the Lofotveggen en route for the narrow and beguiling Raftsundet. A fifth has left the Arctic city of Tromsø in the direction of Finnmark, a sixth member of the fleet has just rounded Nordkyn, the northernmost point on the European mainland.

At exactly the same time a corresponding fleet is on its way southwards. One is between the fishing villages of Båtsfjord and Berlevåg, one en route for its midnight call at

Tromsø, one is painting its white wake on the waters of Vestfjord, one has crossed the Arctic Circle and left the land of the midnight sun behind, and one is soldiering down the coast of Vestlandet to get to Bergen in time for its next northbound departure.

They are all dotted along the coast like a string of pearls. Eleven ships with 3–400 sailors, depending on the season. A complete little civilian defence system, watching over Norway by day and night. Each ship has two sets of crew. After two round trips they have two trips off. Every other year the ships are taken out of service and into dock. And after a new stroke of paint under the hull, changing a worn-out piston, or a new carpet in the saloon these faithful vessels are again ready to take their place along the coastal route. All the ships take passengers, cargo and vehicles, and every one of them can steam along at 15 knots.

Even though tourists quickly discovered the charm of the coastal steamer, it has never lost its essential quality of belonging to the people who live in the coastal districts. A workhorse for people in the eight counties stretching from Hordaland to the border with Russia. When the coastal steamer is moored at the quayside in Bergen it doesn't cut an imposing figure. But as soon as it casts off to start the journey northwards it seems to grow in stature. For the youngsters on the quay farthest north the coastal steamer

Sheltered among the mountains lies Bergen, the coastel steamer's southern turning point. The southbound calls after 11 days at sea. In a few hours later it will be on its way north again.
(Photo: Olav Midtun)

■

is a huge ocean-going steamship.

Many a young lad who has dreamt of being mate or captain on board has later made that dream come true. But the coastal steamer has always been the workplace for many women along the coast. It is said that in the old days mothers in Finnmark would threaten their daughters: "If you don't behave yourself, you won't be a stewardess on the coastal steamer when you grow up!"

Many of the crewmembers have an intense sense of loyalty towards their ship. Year in year out they make their way up and down the beautiful but forbidding coastline – in the same ship. Many have rejected the lure of international shipping

and kept to coastal waters. They've got it in their blood. If you put one of these to skipper a vessel trafficking the Mediterranean you can be pretty sure the ship would end up on the coast of Finnmark!

Many of the passengers also have problems "breaking the habit". The M/S "Harald Jarl" had a lady fan who did the round trip 30 times. "Nordnorge" had an admirer in Sweden who did the same trip

80 times. Not to mention the man who refused to go ashore: he took three trips in a row aboard the same ship and ended up demanding to be given some overalls and a paintbrush so that he could help the men on the deck with the spring-cleaning!

But in the final instance the coastal steamer is an integral part of life along the coast. Though people can now choose to travel by car or by plane, they retain their unswerving faith in the eleven ships.

Witness the words in the local newspaper "Finnmarken" after the first storms one winter: "Planes, buses and cars had to throw in the towel. But the coastal steamer, as usual, braved the elements."

100 YEARS OF SAILING

People thought he had lost his senses, and insurance companies hesitated to cover his venture. But Richard With, the experienced Norwegian sea captain, knew what he was doing when he put forth his revolutionary idea: he wanted to start a steamship route running between northern and southern Norway; one that would sail night and day all year round.

From the time of the Vikings – and even before – there had been shipping along the Norwegian coast. In fact, it was the channels along the coast that had given the country its name, "the north way" – Norway.

The Gulf Stream keeps harbours ice-free year round even though the northernmost tip of Norway lies as close to the North Pole as Point Barrow, Alaska.

Down through the centuries there had also been lively merchant traffic between northern Norway and the export city of Bergen in the south. Each spring and fall skiffs from the north rode the waves south, filled to the brim with dried fish.

■

Captain Richard With (right) was the man with a daring plan – a plan which he made a reality.

■

D/S "Vesteraalen", the first coastal steamer, arriving at Bodø on its virgin voyage in 1893, half-an-hour ahead of schedule!

Tourists discovered the coastal steamer early on. First to come were the British.
The coastal steamer made Norway famous as "The Land of the Midnight Sun", and the number of foreign tourists is steadily increasing.

■

They returned home again, their holds bulging with flour, syrup, tar and salt – and perhaps a few metres of lovely dress fabric for a waiting sweetheart. In addition, the ship also took on one or two passengers.

The mail, too, had a history of sea travel before the advent of the coastal steamer. Relay teams of determined men in "Nordland-boats" rowed mail from Helgeland, just below the Arctic Circle, to as far north as Finnmark. But wind and weather were fickle allies. Once, a clergyman bound for East Finnmark with his wife and flock of children spent ten months on the journey from the capital city of Oslo, a distance of 1600 nautical miles. During the winter months important letters destined for

Finnmark were sent in duplicate for security: one copy by boat, and one by mountain post through Sweden.

As early as the 1830's, the first steamship, "Prinds Gustav", headed up the Nordland channel. In Lofoten this new creature was met with fear and trepidation; as if such a smoke-belching monster would scare schools of cod far out to

∎

MIS "Nordkapp" is one of the latest additions to the fleet. Here seen cruising along the coast of Vestlandet on a bracing August evening. Ahead lie the rough seas of Hustadvika and the port of Kristiansund, famed for its dried cod.

sea, and must surely be in league with the devil himself. In Tromsø, on the other hand, the steamer was met with toasts, public speeches, and a civic ball.

"Prinds Gustav" sailed only in the summer, and its first call in the spring was a major event in the north, as much a cause for celebration as the return of the sun. And now, in addition to the annual arrival of winged migrants, northern Norway had its first steam-driven visitor.

As time passed, other ships joined the "Prinds" in the fleet. Both the parliament and the authorities saw the steamship as a means to unite Norwegians in the north and south as one people. Consequently, the first ships were the property of the state. But soon private interests

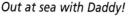

Out at sea with Daddy!

entered the scene, and in the last half of the century, with state backing, they assumed control of the line.

Gradually the size of the fleet increased, and with each new ship the route expanded to include other ports of call. In the south, Bergen was included; and in the north, Vadsø became a summer stop. Naturally, the demand for its services increased. The first ships had been intended for mail and passengers. Soon the amount of cargo grew, the tempo increased, and sailings became more frequent. However, it still took between

nine and ten days to travel from Bergen to Hammerfest, a distance of 900 nautical miles. And even during the light months of the year, there were only weekly departures from Bergen.

There was still one crucial problem to be solved. In the fall and winter, the ships had to lie at anchor at night. This is where Captain With came forth with his great idea.

In addition to his own thorough knowledge of the Norwegian coast, he was fortunate to have at his side one of the coast's most competent pilots,

Anders Holte. During the daytime voyages, Holte had meticulously noted all courses and times. Thus it was just a matter of setting out in the dark of night, follow clock and compass, log and navigation notes.

On Sunday, July 2, 1893, the white pioneer ship, "Vesteraalen", bedecked with flags, glided out of Trondheim. It was a victory ride unlike any other, and the date is etched into the memories of natives of the north as their own national day. Northern Norway had gotten its "hurtigrute", its own coastal steamer.

The venture enjoyed one success after the other, and just before World War II the project was completed. From 1936 on, there were daily sailings from Bergen all the way to Kirkenes.

Then came the war. Five years of German occupation took its toll on the fleet. Half of the ships were lost. At one point, two ships were sunk in the space of two days. North of Hammerfest, the "Richard With", named after the pioneer, went down in 50 seconds, taking 97 lives.

After this, polar vessels were used between Tromsø and

Autumn is a season of beauty on the coastal steamer. Morning glory at Torvik. Next port of call – Ålesund!

■

Kirkenes. This "substitute line" carried 25,000 passengers and large amounts of essential supplies to and from the fishing settlements along the Finnmark coast.

Then came peace and the postwar years. The fleet was built up anew, and in 1964, the last ship of the second genera-

tion of this fleet joined the endless, moving chain of coastal steamers along the coast and the rebuilding phase was over. By the turn of the century, the fourth generation of ships since the war will have taken their place in the fleet. The first of the new ships, "Kong Harald", arrived in 1993.

THE OUVERTURE

Two types of passengers can be found boarding a ship. For one type, the ship is a means to an end: reaching a destination as soon as possible. For the other type, the trip is an end in itself. If you are of the first type, you quickly find your cabin or a place to sit in the lounge and spend most of your time watching the clock and re-checking your estimated time of arrival. If you are of the second type, you forget time, and hope the journey never ends. A delayed departure or minor engine trouble – only *minor* engine trouble – reducing

Floating bird sanctuaries in the evening sun. – No matter what ship you sail on, the experience is the same! The dock at Rørvik.

■

Bergen – once a busy port in the Hansa League, Norway's capital, and Scandinavia's largest trade centre. Now a charming blend of old and new. The city's oldest building, Saint Mary's Church, dating from the 12th century, is surrounded by old and new houses, in a style characteristic of Bergen.

your speed a few knots, fills your heart with childlike glee. You know you will get to spend even more time on board!

When I first travelled on the coastal steamer, I always brought along a good novel. I now leave my novels at home. So much is happening all the time, I never get a chance to open a book anyway.

As a young man, I worked as a travel guide on a coastal steamer. One time we had an overworked shirt manufacturer from Oslo onboard. His wife, in an attempt to prevent him

■

*At crack of dawn on the first morning out, a coastal steamer passes under
the 860-meter high, awe-inspiring rock face, Hornelen (next page), and
then sails up the narrow and temperamental Skatestraumen straits.
On this day in May, small farms and fishing huts along the shores
sparkle in the early morning sun.*

from having a heart attack, had
convinced him to take an
eleven-day round-trip cruise
on the coastal steamer.

The first few days he was
like a tiger in a cage. When he
wasn't restlessly pacing about
the ship, he could be found
with the radio operator, bor-
rowing the phone. He had only
one thought on his mind – he
wanted to get this trip over and
return to his shirts.

But little by little, something
happened. His tempo slowed,
he forgot all about the telepho-
ne, and let shirts be shirts. He
had been swept along by the
ship's rhythms. He followed
carefully every manoeuvre on
board. Every time the ship
approached or departed a dock,
he could be found leaning over
the railing. He followed with
the curiosity of a young boy
the loading and unloading of

cargo, and kept track of who
came and went over the gangplank.

When he disembarked on
the eleventh day, both he and
his wife looked as if they had
been on their second honey-
moon. Out of this overworked
factory owner, an authentic
coastal steamer fan was born!
He was already looking forward to his next trip.

■

No rest to be had ... there's always something new to see!

It begins the minute you cast off in Bergen and sail out into the night. You have barely managed to find your way around onboard before you feel you simply must go on deck – just to watch. Astern is the city itself, a glowing amphitheatre watching the ship wend its way through the archipelago. Then the ship eases into the sea lane where it is protected by a row of low barren islands, and

begins the long and arduous journey north.

Before you turn in for the night, you will have sailed into the Norwegian oil age. An hour after leaving Bergen a sea of light intrudes upon the darkness as you pass a gigantic oil terminal. A bit further, over the starboard bow, one of northern Europe's largest oil refineries, Mongstad, will

light up the night yet again.

To avoid being totally sated your first day on board, you might consider sleeping through the night call at Florø. Save this charming white-washed west-country village for the trip south. But don't sleep too long. Early – very early – the next morning, at six a.m., you will sail in under the awe-inspiring Hornelen, a 860-meter-high wall of rock that drops vertically, and threateningly, into the sea.

Because of the danger of rock slides, we are not allowed to sound the horn while passing under the Hornelen. There is a crack in the rock mass which grows larger from year to year, and one day this colossus will crash down. The officers on the bridge cast a humble glance upward as they round it, and hope they are way up north or have retired the day this giant finally decides to topple into the sea.

Soon they have other things to think about. Just after passing Hornelen, the ship heads up the narrow and swift Skatestraumen. No sooner have we conquered these turbulent currents, when a pyramid-shaped mountaintop rises up ahead. At its base, windowpanes glisten in the morning sun. This is the port of Måløy, and before the gong sounds for breakfast, you will have managed to berth and cast off again at one of Norway's largest and most productive centres for the processing and export of fish.

In addition to its fishing enterprise, Måløy also has a place in the history of the war. On December 27, 1941, Allied commando forces attacked. One of Norway's greatest war heroes, Captain Martin Linge, led the Norwegian division and fell in the fierce battle.

North of Måløy, the ship hits open sea, but it doesn't stay there for long. A scant two hours later and you are back in the sheltered waters of the archipelago. You will have also sailed past Norway's westernmost point: robust, windswept Stadtlandet, reaching like a fist

out into the sea, as if it were trying to protect the little community of Ervik.

Rounding Stadt is one of the most powerful experiences of the trip. The ship sails close in under these rounded, windswept mountains. If there are

heavy seas, you may, if you wish, remain in your bunk for the duration of this «memorable experience». But if you want the «real» experience, put on all your warmest clothes and place yourself as far forward as possible on the leeward side of

One hour after Måløy, the coastal steamer rounds Norway's westernmost point – Stadt. The Stadt sea is the first of the six stretches of open sea on the 1250-nautical-mile voyage north.

■

the ship, and ride out its dance around Norway's westernmost point. If you thrust your head forward, sea spray will provide a refreshing shower.

The Stadt sea is the first of six areas of open sea the ship will traverse on its journey northward. Even though it can be crossed quickly, seamen have great respect for this particular stretch of unruly seas. Here the Atlantic is at your doorstep, with its perilous sea-bed adding to the fury of the sea when the southwesterly storms roll on.

Nothing stops the costal steamer. Not even on the last night of 1992, when winds of 120 knots – nearly two times hurricane force – cast themselves upon the coast of western Norway in the worst hurricane in memory.

When the Armageddon was over, parts of the western coast looked like a battlefield. Houses were swept into the sea, cars and camping caravans were smashed, entire farms were reduced to rubble. The roof of the church in Kristiansund was swept away. The ravaged city, which lay in darkness due to a power failure, was declared a disaster area.

The storm also resulted in dramatic rescue operations at sea. Several ships went aground. The wreckage of pleasure boats as well as fishing vessels lay scattered among the rocks along the coastline. Near Ålesund, a thousand ton trawler was thrown onto dry land. Three hundred thousand salmon escaped from their breeding nets. News flashes announced the cancellation of flight and boat departures, and people were asked to remain indoors. But there were no news flashes regarding the coastal steamer. It sailed.

The old M/S "Nordstjernen" was southbound that New Year's Eve. It had served as a "Christmas Boat" on its way north and was almost fully-booked with round-trip passengers – Swedes, Danes, Germans, Belgians, Scotsmen, Frenchmen, and Norwegians. At the stroke of midnight, she sailed into the harbour at Ålesund and was greeted by a sky full of fireworks. The captain responded by sending a blast of the ship's horn echoing through the mountains. Champagne was served on the afterdeck, and earlier the guests had warmed up with a gala dinner and a

Rounding this distinctive headland, Stadtlandet, is an exciting way to start the day. To make the most of this experience, go on deck, let the wind rush through your hair, and watch the sea break upon islets and rocky outcroppings; or just stand at the railing and study the waves! The seas are seldom perfectly calm. Within two hours, you will have returned to the sheltered waters of the archipelago.

■

The coastal steamer is more than north Norway and the midnight sun. The west coast has a charm of its own, and each season its beauty and drama.

Left: Flåvær lighthouse near Torvik on an April morning.

Christmas day – southward bound a few hours from Bergen. The low winter sun spreads a golden glow over the islands along the route. Two days to the north there was no sun at all!

■

April in Ålesund. A northbound coastal steamer at the dock. The stopover allows you time to reach – on foot or by taxi – the top of Aksla, a rocky outcrop lying within the city. Once there, you can enjoy one of the most impressive panorama views of the entire voyage.

A hot summer's day in Molde fjord. Molde is famed for its jazz festival and its summer roses, but it is beautiful in the winter too. Molde patriots can boast of no fewer than 87 snow-capped peaks that can be seen from their city.

Polonaise through the lounges.

Four hours later, the hurricane was upon them – right in the middle of the Stadt sea. The storm approached from the aft. Even at greatly reduced engine speeds the ship was being bowled along at 20 knots – a feat that undoubtedly qualifies for the Guinness Book of World Records.

At 1350 hours the next day the northbound M/S "Nordnorge", the forerunner of today's ship, cast off from Måløy. By then the hurricane had had time to properly whip up the Stadt sea, and the waves varied from 20 to 30 meters in height.

First Mate Dybedal from Måløy stands with one hand on the manoeuvring control. The "Nordnorge" is working hard. The seas, which are becoming stronger and stronger, wash over the deck, and occasionally a breaker crashes over the bridge, flooding the windows with saltwater and blocking visibility.

Being a veteran of the coastal steamer, he knows the Stadt sea. It has been his neighbour all his life, and he has crossed it in all types of weather. But as the waves become larger and harder to climb, he begins to wonder if he has

ever seen the Stadt like this before.

With 3500 horsepower in its belly, the "Nordnorge" braces itself and charges up each new wave, increasing its speed as it climbs. Then it descends to the depths of the wave at a third of that speed. Each confrontation with a large wave is a contest between man and the sea. Even though this first mate is soon to retire, inside him there is still a young boy alive and well. He is aware of the fact that he likes to hone himself by challenging the forces of nature, and he feels a child-like thrill in his heart. He suddenly realises that he is sing-

ing a song he learned as a young boy in school; a song that is almost the national anthem of the west-country, "Among mountains and hills facing the sea . . ."

Back in calm waters, enroute to Ålesund, he remarks to the pilot over a cup of piping hot coffee, "If this isn'a fantastic life, I don't know what is!"

Passengers too can revel in the joys of a turbulent sea. One time when we were north-bound over the Stadt sea in a gale I caught sight of a figure standing in the sea spray – a lone woman stood along the railing, as far aft as possible...

hanging on for dear life. Was she seasick? Did she need help? I balance myself and move cautiously toward her. When I reach her, a heavily-clad woman nearing 80, smiles radiantly and nods toward a mountain of a wave that looks like it will engulf the both of us. "Ich bin aus Berlin. I love standing here in this weather!" "Why?", I ask. "Because, when I stand here, the distance between life and death is so short," she replies.

THROUGH THE GATEWAY TO THE LAND OF THE MIDNIGHT SUN

On the old "Midnatsol" (Midnight Sun) on a grey December day. The ship, a gorgeous Italian built in Ancona, was one of the first new ships to join the fleet after the war. By now it has found its way to the scrapyard and been made into nails.

We cast off at noon and sail out into the fjord, with the southbound ship in our wake. In the past, ships going north and those going south departed at the same time from Trondheim. You could always tell them apart: those going south, having just unloaded fish from northern Norway, floated jauntily over the surface of the water. Within a day she would be moored in Bergen, refilling her holds with vegetables, fruit, flour, margarine, clothing, soap powder, and machinery destined for people all along the coast.

I take a stroll on the deck. An ice-encrusted ladder leads up to the bridge. Astern lies the thousand-year-old city of Trondheim shrouded in clouds of frost. On both sides of the fjord are communities of farm-

Big 'uns and little 'uns all aboard – and full steam ahead!

*Past and present side by side.
Nidaros Cathedral – Norway's largest
and most famous medieval building –
and Ravnkloa, where local fishermen
supply the citizens with
their catches direct from the boats.*

■

*Every day at 12 noon the northbound
steamer casts off from Trondheim.
For the first couple of hours it sails
past low hills and rolling farmland –
a landscape seen nowhere else
along the route.*

Sunset at Folla north of Trondheim.
Thousands of beacons and light-
houses lead the vessels safely up
and down the rugged coast.
An hour or two in open sea,
and there is a weather-beaten
lighthouse showing the way to
another port of call.

■

steads frozen to a blue-white.
The December day lies still and
cold over the landscape.

The door to the bridge wing
is partially open, and the temptation to defy the frosted-over
NO ENTRY sign is too much.
I poke my nose over the forward bulwark; a cold gust of
wind almost brings tears to my
eyes.

Through a window in the
door to the bridge, I see the
pilot, warm and snug, pacing
the deck, his hands held behind
his back. Back and forth, back
and forth, like the pendulum of
a clock. There is a hint of gray
in his hair, and three gold bands
decorate the sleeve of his jacket.
He must surely have many
kilometres of pacing behind

him since first becoming a pilot
along the coast.

Shivering, I start my retreat
to the interior of the ship,
regaining some degree of
warmth when I stop for a
moment in the crosscurrent of
warm air streaming up through
the doorway to the engine
room. The aroma of freshly-

poached fish wafts up from the
galley a few decks below, and I
go down and stick my head
through the hatch. The cook
promises freshly-caught cod for
dinner. Here in the galley, a
transistor radio has been strap-
ped down to the countertop,
and the strains of a pop melody
blend with the steam from a pot
of potatoes boiling away on the
stove.

By the time we have left the
Trondheim fjord, we have
managed to enjoy dinner and
the sunset. With the southbound ship still visible in our
wake, we round the approach
light at Agdenes. But it is time
to part company. We turn to
starboard and bear west.
Cutting past a hunch-backed

The northbound "Vesteraalen" threads its way through the narrow and convoluted Stoksundet sound north of Trondheim. Cameras are in action on all the decks!!

■

islet, we set course for the north. To starboard lies Ør-landet, an area as flat as a pancake and bleached by frost. It looks like the brim of a hat; the crown of the hat being the smooth, rounded mountains further inland. Astern, the sun sets over curvaceous mountains. South of us in the sea lane, the southbound coastal steamer is lit up against the black backdrop of land.

The red-painted Kjeung-skjær lighthouse sweeps close by us on the port side; the islet it stands on so tiny it looks as if the watchtower is sticking right up out of the sea. In the past, there was always a light shining from the third floor window. The lighthouse-keeper actually

lived in the tower; there wasn't room for both a lighthouse and a residence on this little piece of rock out here in the sea. Twice a day, the waves of a passing coastal steamer washed the keepers waterfront and the steps to his landing. But the keepers have since been replaced by technology, and like so many of Norway's lighthouses, Kjeung-skjær is operated by remote control from the mainland.

The seaway along the coast of Trøndelag is a dangerous thoroughfare. Many a cargo ship has gone down in bad weather. When a storm rages mercilessly, or the fog is as thick as pea soup, a coastal steamer has been known to depart this troubled channel for the open sea.

We sail in still waters and travel in an inner sea lane as darkness slowly settles upon us. We creak along among scerries, points, and islands. A lighthouse here, a blinking light there, a buoy now and again. The pilot glances at his watch, checks the compass, examines the radar screen. A few minutes on one course, then a little to the starboard, then to the port side. Straight ahead for awhile, and then to starboard again.

I am in heaven! I have been allowed into the inner sanctum. I stand aft of the bridge and follow the progress of the voyage. I watch the pilot's movements. It is as if he has all the time in the world as he saunters over to the binoculars, lifts them to his eyes, and scouts – not ahead of us, but along the side of the craft. "15 starboard," he calls out, suddenly. I approach the window of the bridge, and see the silhouette of a spar slice along the side of the boat. The ship heels over a bit in response to his command. I walk to the other side. The outlines of an islet brush past us. We've encountered a narrowing of the passage, only a few vessels wide, but then the channel opens up again. The ship rights itself after the turn and ploughs northward again.

Thus, slowly but surely, the ship works its way north in the evening hours; navigating the narrow and convoluted Stoksundet sound with restraint, then bursting out of this mountainscape and speeding toward the open sea of Folla. At about 6 p.m. we see a good-sized lighthouse on the starboard side. There is but a narrow little passage left before we are on our way to Folla and the open sea.

She holds the same course for three quarters of an hour, and by then she's cleared the shoals and scerries, and changes course heading northeast. At this point a lighthouse should appear off the bow on the port side. It will be Gjæslingen, the approach light to the next port of call, Rørvik. Once it has been spotted, it's a straight shot to Rørvik, passing under the impressive suspension bridge and then

on to the pier. In the course of two hours, we have traversed the Folla sea.

A captain I know used to say that nothing was as beautiful as the sunset over Folla – or as mischievous.

Folla has many faces. She shows the least beautiful when she has been stirred up by a southwester. She makes ugly faces, foams maniacally at the mouth, and bares a thousand jagged teeth. Folla is a greedy sea. She has taken her toll of ships for as long as ships have sailed these waters. Sloops, cargo ships and good-sized freighters

have been her victims.

Coastal steamers have always managed to escape. True enough, they have often had to brace themselves against a storm and charge forward, often tolerating a wet slap in the face by an angry sea. But they have always made it into port. Because of this, no one in the tiny fishing settlement of Rørvik believed what they heard one Sunday evening in October of 1962 when rumours began to circulate that a coastal steamer had gone down outside their village.

The next morning the flags

did indeed fly at half-mast all over Rørvik. The first bulletins regarding casualties had come in. Throughout the day, boat upon boat slid into the dock bearing corpses.

Three, five, ten, twenty – and there would be even more. As evening approached, a fishing smack glided into the harbour with a heavy heart. It had thirteen more victims onboard. At the docks, silent groups of people had gathered, devastated by sorrow. Mothers with children, men with weather-beaten faces who were well acquainted with life's hardships. All were

Left: Sailing in to Rørvik – gateway to the marine highway north.

The coastal steamer has a special place in the heart of Rørvik. Every year the town honours the fleet with a "Coastal Steamer Day". Northbound and southbound ships call at the harbour at the same time, making the quayside bustle with life and activity.
(Photo: Knut Hjelvik)

incapable of understanding.

But dispersed among private homes and boarding houses in the area, were the 48 that Folla had not taken, and each and every one had their own personal tale to tell.

The unthinkable had happened. The ship, which had been 12 nautical miles off course for over an hour, had struck a shoal. Forty years have passed since this tragedy and yet even today you will find navigators who hesitate a moment just as they are about to set out for Folla heading north. They stop and remember, and ask themselves for the umpteenth time: How could this have happened?

No one knows the answer. The three men standing on the bridge of the doomed ship that fateful night – the pilot, the helmsman, and the captain – were among the 41 who lost their lives.

The tragedy at Folla that October evening in 1962 is the

Every child's dream – a visit to the navigation bridge! The coastal steamer also serves as a classroom for middle-school students on work-study programs.

■

Just south of Brønnøysund lies the mountain from the myth, Torghatten, complete with its hole! The southbound ships swing to the west so you can capture this natural phenomenon on film.

■

A voyage on the coastal steamer is a journey of unmatched natural beauty. Hour by hour the landscape changes – from massive mountains and open seas to fertile farmlands and idyllic narrow sounds, such as here at Brønnøysund.

most serious shipwreck to occur on a coastal steamer in peacetime. Otherwise, safety has been the trademark of the coastal steamer for as long as it has travelled "Coastal Highway Number 1". The fact that so many ships have sailed up and down this harsh coastline year round for a hundred years with so few accidents is a tribute to good seamanship. It is because of this safety record that the wreck at Folla made such a strong impression on the people of the little community of Rørvik. The unthinkable had happened.

When a ship heads north out of

Rørvik, it has been enroute 48 hours since its departure from Bergen. The narrow, turbulent sound between Rørvik and the mountainous land on the inland side is considered the gateway to the "Nordland route". For those who travel for the experience, and not just to reach their destination, this stretch will mark the beginning of the "days" of staying up all night. There are many of these types of travellers in the summer, and it is this part of the voyage that has made the coastal steamer so famous all over the world.

When you depart from Rørvik, there is still a night's journey before the ship crosses the Arctic Circle and glides into the land of the midnight sun. Those who actually wish to sleep through the night, would do well to pull their blankets way up over their heads. Dark nights are a thing of the past.

In their attempts to "sell" the area of Norway called "Nordkalotten" (the "scull cap" in Norwegian), the tourist offices often entice customers with the promise of the midnight sun. They would do better to market the light: the vigilant, yet tentative, night light that gently covers landscape and seascape, even entering dwellings, like a gentle, ephemeral veil.

This other-worldly light is perhaps not as easy to capture with a camera lens as is the midnight sun, and thus it may not make it to the travel posters, but it penetrates deeper, and captures one's soul.

The words "Nordland route" call to mind the legend about the King of Lofoten called

Vågekallen who had a lustful maniac named Hestmannen (the Horse Man) for a son. Inland lived the king of the Sulis with his seven lovely daughters. One time when the seven of them – this was when they still had the beautiful Lekamøya among them – were visiting a woman who lived by the sea, they decided to bathe naked one evening. The lecherous Hestmannen caught sight of them, and Lekamøya, who was incredibly beautiful, was too much of a temptation for this boy from Lofoten. At midnight he saddled his horse – this being long before the days of the coastal steamer – and galloped across the fjord to capture her.

When the sisters saw him coming they ran as fast as they could down the channel toward the south. At Brønnøysund lived the king of the Sømnafjellet mountain, who was awakened by the commotion. When he saw the raging Hestmannen lift his bow and send an arrow after these fleeing beauties, he tossed his hat in the path of the arrow. And at that very moment, the sun rose.

Thus it has become a tenet of Norwegian folklore that trolls cannot survive in the sun. The moment the sun appears, a troll will turn to stone. Today, Vågekallen, Hestmannen, Lekamøya, and several others have taken the guise of popular landmarks along the coastal route.

Just south of the port of Sandnessjøen live the beautiful sisters – seven mountains all in a row – remembering their days in the world of trolls. The hat belonging to the king of the

Sømnafjellet at Brønnøysund, complete with the hole the arrow made in it, is now a mountain called "Torghatten", and it lies just south of Brønnøysund. Off the port side two hours north of Rørvik, we can see the fair Lekamøya. And just over the bow is the easily identifiable Brønnøy king's hat. For the next 24 hours, we will be sailing in the land of legends.

A night in Helgeland is more than an encounter with mythology. It is also a gliding state of transition to a totally different type of scenery. The langu-

*Early in the morning during the summer season, just after crossing the Artic Circle, the ship slows down and stops.
A ferry comes alongside and picks up passengers for an optional excursion to the Svartisen, Norway's second largest glacier.*

■

*Summer night on the threshold of the kingdom of the midnight sun. Northbound steamer leaves Brønnøysund.
(Photo: Vivi Brit Espolin Johnson)*

id, rounded mountain areas surrounding the Trondheim fjord and spreading north from there gradually give way to stately, towering rock masses. Peaks and pinnacles appear here and there; a patch of snow may catch your eye. It is in Helgeland that the natural beauty of the land begins to show its might. Out toward the open sea, islet upon islet form a long band as far as the eye can see. You have taken your first step into the first of northern Norway's three counties. "Nordland" is the name.

If the narrow sound at Rørvik is the gateway to the Nordland channel, then the town of Brønnøysund is at the eye of the needle. At midnight, the ship heads up past Torghatten and sets about threading its way through the narrowest passage of the entire voyage, the narrow and winding approach to Brønnøysund.

In days gone by, in the dark of winter an old woman guided them through. She lived on the islet where the channel narrows to the proverbial bottleneck and starts to zigzag. With only her sheep for company, she steadfastly refused to move from this tiny grass-covered islet on which she had been born.

Every night before going to bed she would light the outdoor lantern, which is effect functioned as a lighthouse in itself, operating from her humble little sway-backed cottage.

As soon as the ship has slipped past her cottage, it reduces its speed. On the bridge, intense concentration reigns. Music is turned down, idle talk stops. Two pairs of very alert eyes track the ship's every move.

Soon the ship sails in under a bridge, and a long flat island suddenly appears on the port side. Houses, in a tight line, and each with a well-kept patch of garden reaching all the way

The coast of Helgeland, with its imposing mountains, its myriad of islets and narrow passages, is worth a trip on its own. South of Sandnessjøen are the Seven Sisters – a range of mountain peaks famed in Norse mythology. On fair weather days it's difficult to tear yourself away from the railing.
(Photo, top: Knut Hjelvik)

down to the rocky beach, appear. The ship passes so close that you could take inventory of their living-rooms, if you were so inclined.

The ship willingly responds to the movements of the helm, listing from side to side to the tune of the rudder. It tilts gent-

ly in the turns, sails tauntingly close to a succession of islets, and within a few meters of the rocks. Each turn brings us the length of the ship closer to Brønnøysund. But the narrowest passage, the last little stretch, is still to come.

Suddenly, we are there. I go

to the railing, look over the side and see bottom; rush over to the opposite side only to see the light reflected from the sandy bottom there also. And dead ahead? An islet with an iron spar atop it coming right at us. We're heading straight for terra firma at a speed of five knots.

But no. At the last minute the ship heels over, the result of a hard rudder to starboard. A cairn, whitewashed with seagull droppings, swoops by within spitting distance. But what about the islet with the iron stake? You run back to the other side and see that it appears to be

Southbound along the Helgelands coast on a warm summer day – balm for the soul.

■

■

Preceding pages:
It is not as barren north of the Arctic Circle as many believe. Here is the channel as seen from the fertile island of Meløy, outside of Ørnes. It's possible to "raid the beaches" under-way – just lay over a day or two and catch the next boat.

■

I'm always wondering – what lies just round the next headland? But of course if you're a Londoner, you take this matter-of-factly – at least at teatime.

rapidly approaching the stern, which is in the middle of its turn. Then, at the last minute, the ship rights herself again. A turn of the rudder toward port, and the coastguard's iron stake squeezes by and disappears behind us.

The pilot has completed his task. Ahead lies the open harbour, and a dock. This ten minute long navigational feat is over, and this spellbound passenger finds himself quaking in his boots. The ship's horn resounds through the night: one long, one short, and another long. Natives of Brønnøysund

may not even have stirred in their sleep. They know this sound from a thousand other nights: the northbound ship is approaching the dock.

A bit further north in the seaway, the legendary Dønna-mannen lies on his back snoring. His chin, mouth, nose and

An early August morning as a southbound ship approaches Ørnes – one of the most beautiful ports of call on the trip. The island of Meløya, which gives the district its name, can be seen in the background.

forehead are silhouetted against the tomato-red night sky. As soon as the ship is well off-shore, it sets its course for the hollow of his throat. If visibility is good, you will see the "Seven Sisters" mountain chain – your friends from the legend – off the starboard bow. And by the time you take your morning coffee in the dining room, you will have passed the Arctic Circle. You have entered the land of the midnight sun.

■

Some people know how to take things easy ...

■

Camping out on deck, with a sleeping-bag,
a pack of sandwiches ... and a good novel.

34 calls each way.
Every few hours the ship opens
its gates and lets out a stream
of travellers eager to explore
a new port of call.

■

... whilst others are busy trying to see a bit of everything!

■

The northbound steamer has crossed the Arctic Circle, and speeds on towards Bodø, whilst the passengers enjoy the sun of a mid-June morning.

LOFOTEN DEAD AHEAD!

There are few places along the coast where the coastal steamer is as much a part of the life of the city as in Bodø. At high noon, the busiest time of the day, a northbound ship sails into the mouth of the harbour, takes a victory lap, and announces its arrival to the residents. Then it pulls up alongside the dock at the new terminal, just a ten minute walk from the centre of town.

From 12 to 3 p.m. the dock bustles with activity. Red and yellow lifts work like busy ants carting crates of apples, sacks of potatoes, colour TVs, bicycles, and iron goods in and out of the ship's belly.

Passengers of all ages, and all shapes and sizes, move on and off the ship: seasoned fishermen wearing their "city finery" and caps characteristic of their trade; women in kerchiefs who struggle onboard with bags and packages, and cardboard cartons tied up with string. Mothers with children in their arms, teenagers in love, chewing their gum while their cassette players blare at full blast.

At no other port is our departure preceded by so much hectic activity as in Bodø. The state railway line terminates here, and there is also a major airport with direct flights to points north and south.

Passengers stream onboard from both train and plane, and from shopping trips in "the big city". The first 24 hours after our departure from Bodø is the

Mother and child – togetherness on the way north

■

most hectic of the entire trip. In the course of the evening, and during the night, ports of call pop up one after the other.

Never is this poor purser as busy as after the departure from Bodø. A nice bunk to crawl into may also be a necessity for passengers if Vestfjorden, the fourth of the areas of open sea on the voyage, decides to be ornery. Then, even the bravest of soldiers will have to throw in the towel and find refuge in the horizontal position.

Vestfjorden isn't naughty all the time. Try the crossing on a beautiful summer day, or a mag-nificent spring day in March or April. On days such as these, the ship lists toward the sun as passengers flock to the port

■

Leaving Bodø – the capital of Nordland county.
Over half of the city was levelled by German bombs in May of 1940. Today Bodø is a busy trade and administrative centre serving tens of thousands, from the outermost islands of the Lofoten group in the west, to the Swedish border in the east.In the background the peaks of Børvasstindan.

side, three stories of them, and so tightly packed that the ship resembles a kind of bird sanctu-ary floating across the fjord.

Still, despite the fact that the decks are packed, a special sense of calmness settles over the ship on such days. People have had a hot meal, and per-haps enjoyed a beer, as we sailed out of Bodø. There is a feeling of drowsy contentment in the air.

■

Overleaf: A big boat for big scenery! The "Kong Harald" sets out from Bodø enroute to Lofoten.

In the glass-enclosed area on the upper deck, tourists, a warm blanket over their laps, doze, letting the sun warm their faces. They may glance up now and again and glimpse a strip of mountain peaks behind the flag at the aft of the ship, or observe a seagull swooping down from the top of a mast, threatening to discharge a bomb!

On a lower deck, a mother nurses her youngest in the gentle breeze, nearby two men sit on a bench and discuss the price of fish, a young boy stands at the railing mesmerised by the swirling wake tumbling out of the propeller. All the

while the pleasant rumbling of the engine plays accompaniment to the flow of human activity onboard, erasing the line of distinction clamour and calm.

By the time we're halfway across the fjord, our friends on the upper deck awaken from their afternoon nap. The sun is

■

Sailing in to Stamsund on a May evening. The ship eases in only feet away from the rocky shoreline. Further north, one of the peaks of the Lofoten range soars a thousand metres straight up out of the sea.

no longer warm, and they crane their necks and scan the horizon over the railing, where light glints off a mirror-like sea.

Ahead of us lies what appears to be a vision! Like the blade of a saw, each of its teeth biting into the clear blue heavens, the Lofoten Wall looms up before us. The ship heads straight toward this wall of mountain. Four hours out of Bodø, she glides into the shade of these black precipices. She rounds an islet, and straight ahead a little harbour opens up in the midst of the rock face, revealing a settlement. On an old warehouse

the word STAMSUND is written. One of Lofoten's largest fishing stations, Stamsund was founded at the turn of the century when its first settler literally dynamited his way into the rock mass. Today it is a fourth-generation enterprise.

In the central areas of southern Norway, such as the Oslo area, you have to climb a thousand metres to be in the mountains. But in Lofoten the mountains appear to be already up to their knees in water. And in Svolvær, the ship appears to be heading straight for the mountain.

You stand at the railing and

This sailing Dutchman bathed in the glow of the midnight sun ... seems to have forgotten that it's way past bedtime.

think, this is most certainly going to end in catastrophe! But at the last minute a little slip of a passage opens up between the rock face, which has been scoured to a shine, and a breakwater. The harbour is a tight fit for the coastal steamer, and it is moored almost on top of the town square.

At ten o'clock in the evening, 72 hours since its departure from Bergen, the ship casts off from Svolvær enroute to Stokmarknes. Ahead lies what qualifies as one of the highlights of the trip: the 26-kilometre-long journey through the narrow

Stowaways. Seagulls faithfully trail the ship, hoping for a kind-hearted chef.

■

A southbound ship on the Vestfjord in the midnight sun. In the background, the Lofoten Wall with its garret of pinnacles. This mountain chain stretches 100 kilometres into the sea.

■

Raftsundet sound that binds the island districts of Lofoten and Vesterålen by sea.

Raftsundet retains its magic in any season. Protected as it is on both sides by thousand-metre-high peaks, it reminds one of a boulevard. The ship glides along as if on a tranquil mountain river at the base of a valley.

This leg of the journey is so special that even the crew, who have travelled this stretch so many times before, take a turn on deck to take it in one more time. Why? The secret is this: Raftsundet will never be the same as the last time you sailed it. Seasons change; light changes; the weather has its moods, and so does the observer.

A spring day, snow-covered mountains silhouetted against a fiery evening sky; summer, with deep green mountain slopes so perfectly reflected in the surface of the water that the pilot has to check twice to distinguish between land and sea; autumn, these same slopes ablaze with crimson with just a sprinkling of snow on the mountaintops; and a winter night sparkling in the moonlight when the ship sails as if over a silver plate – all of these are Raftsundet.

During the light season, the ship takes a detour a little ways up the sound and sails into Trollfjorden. When the ship glides in under a several-hund-red-metre-high vertical rock-face, and so close that we are forbidden to sound the ship's

The final journey to Stokmarknes.

Photo at right: In the evening twilight, Svolvær, the "captital" of the Lofoten area, takes the coastal steamer in its embrace. First a southbound ship, and then a few hours later, a northbound. From February to April the fishing industry makes its mark on the city. Fishing vessels hasten in and out of the harbour, and the streets and dock area bustle with activity.

horn for fear of slides, it turns quiet on deck. People bend their heads as far back as possible, and take a few steps back from the railing, just to be on the safe side.

When the ship begins to – very carefully – swing around here at the innermost reach of the fjord, still under this awesome peak, easing its bow along the side of the rock face, there are not a few on deck who forget all about finding their cameras, and instead look

around for the nearest lifeboat.

With still a few feet between the mountain and the bow, the engines are reversed, stopping all movement, and the boat slowly begins to vibrate. It is the mate on the bridge who has applied the brakes, and he looks back to make sure that he doesn't run the aft of the ship aground.

He steers the ship clear, as if it were a toy boat, then through the narrow mouth of the fjord and back to Raftsundet and the

sea lane. We leave behind us the arm of the fjord that many consider the highlight of the entire voyage.

For the fishermen in the north, Trollfjorden calls to mind anything but tourism. On occasion Lofoten cod have gotten confused and swum into this two-kilometre-long and very narrow fjord, providing a bountiful fishing ground indeed for some lucky fishermen.

Trollfjorden has achieved even greater renown for Johan

Lofoten in winter. Skerries scrubbed clean; barren islets; precipitous, snow-covered mountainsides – and a fishing vessel cutting through the breakers on its way to the fishing grounds. April in Kabelvåg – the oldest fishing station in the Lofoten islands. Founded in the 12th century, Kabelvåg is well worth a visit while the ship is moored at Svolvær.

Bojer's novel, "The Last Viking". A classic of Norwegian literature, it has been translated into a number of languages. Bojer provides a lively account of the dramatic "Battle of Trollfjord" in 1880 in which the old ways and new technology clashed. An army of small fishermen in rowboats and sailboats launched a doomed attack on new intruders: steam-driven fishing boats that had blocked the entrance to the fjord and were in the process of reeling in huge catches.

Every once in a while a lonely house pops up along the eastern shore as the ship continues its journey up Raftsundet. The mountains gradually flatten out into a tiny little grassy lip of land – with just enough room for a handful of houses along a deserted country road.

Halfway up this sound, "Harald Jarl" once had a best friend. It was a woman on the shore who initiated this nighttime flirtation; blinking her bedroom lights when she saw her favourite northbound boat flash his signal lights down the channel. "Harald Jarl" would reply by bathing both the old woman and her house in a flood of searchlights. They "carried on" like this for several years until one evening the little white-washed house lay in darkness. The old woman had departed this earthly paradise.

For people along this small

Just ask the tour guide! In the tourist season, he or she is awake day and night – and used to answering the most incredible questions.

■

Right: "M/S Nordnorge" sailing north from Svolvær toward Raftsundet and Trollfjorden – the mighty highlight of the voyage. August an hour before midnight.

■

Being on holiday can be hectic –
especially if one is an artist.
The motifs change from minute
to minute! Being a carefree student
is another story.

■

Overleaf: Inside the Trollfjord.
The "Cathedral" – the powerful
highlight of the voyage.
M/S "Finnmarken", here seen on one
of its last voyages, is now Norway's
largest monument, high and dry
on land at Stokmarknes.

secluded channel, it is the coastal steamer that is the main attraction, not the mountains or the special quality of the moonlight.

The coastal steamer is a breath of fresh air from the world beyond the mountains and the darkness.

Helge is one of the seamen on the new "Midnatsol" (Midnight Sun). He has thirty years' experience along the coast. Three brothers served before him, and their father before them. Helge grew up in Raftsundet, encircled by a wall of mountains. Blocked on every side, there was only one place to look to, the path of the coastal steamer. Twice every 24 hours one of the ships swept by.

On a typical summer day, as 6 o'clock approached, he and his brothers would row as far out in the channel as was safe, and then a little further – enough so that the officer on the bridge would have to sound the horn to clear them away. This made their day. Then they would row for their dear lives back toward land while the sound of the ship's horn echoed through the mountains.

On days when dense fog settled in, they could be found playing on the rocky beach. Suddenly, their play would stop, they would straighten up and listen to the swishing sounds and the rumbling of a ship's engine coming from somewhere out in the channel.

They could almost picture for themselves the outlines of a black hull – the coastal steamer on its way south.

Winter days; the dark months. The coastal steamer represented dreams and adventure. The channel lay there, sombre and threatening. Then the ship would arrive, a glowing vision gliding through the darkness. Sometimes there appeared to be two ships, as lanterns, salon windows, and small round portholes were reflected in the smooth surface of the waters.

The coastal steamer is like a magic castle to the children of this secluded settlement, cut off from the world. Is it any wonder that one or another of them would wish themselves onboard?

NORWAY IN MINIATURE

«Tromsø – still a 'beauty shock'!" wrote my wife in her diary one February.

A grey-blue day in January just after the first of the year found us on the coastal steamer, travelling north to live in Tromsø, the "capital" of northern Norway, and the world's northernmost university town.

After several years as a tour guide in the high season, I had long ago discovered the summer light – the dream light typical of northern Norway – and fallen in love with it. This January journey from Trondheim to Tromsø was my first in the dark months.

This trip helped me to better understand a painter friend of mine from northern Norway who once told me, "It is the light in the dark months that is my light – the September to January light. It is a light that doesn't always come from the sky; but from the landscape. The snow and surf are sources of light. Their gray-blue and sea-green are shades of colour. At this time of year, there is a special mystique in the natural surroundings of northern Norway."

Sailing north on the coastal steamer through winter landscapes allows you to drink in this mystique, and you partake so much more greedily than you would if you were standing in one place. With the alertness of an adventurer you take in each and every permutation of light and colour. And when the northern lights flame up in the heavens, you stand riveted to the railing – until the frost gets to you and sends you back to the lounge to thaw out. Perhaps what the people of northern Norway say is true: Anyone who hasn't experienced the

Left: Under the impressive Vågekallen. High summer in Lofoten.

∎

Rendezvous at Vestfjorden. For the crew there's always a familiar face on other ships of the fleet. A sweetheart, perhaps?

∎

Tromsø, also called "the Artic City", is the capital of the North, and can proudly boast of having the northernmost university in the world.

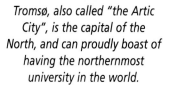

North toward Tromsø the mountains climb more than a thousand metres up from the shipping channel. The coastal steamer sails in the midst of this mountainscape – an eldorado for outdoor enthusiasts. Here, in early May.

The meeting of two seasons – autumn's blazing farewell; winter's first sprinkling of snow. The city of Tromsø is situated on an island. This is the residents' view to the west, on a September day.

■

dark months, hasn't really experienced northern Norway.

But they speak with a forked tongue. If the dark months in the north offer such beauty and mysticism, it follows that there would be more nights of staying awake – even for many of the natives. People from southern Norway, especially teachers and health workers, often accept jobs in the north. But it is not uncommon that they have to pack their bags and move south again, the darkness having robbed them of their sleep.

Troms is the middle of the three northern counties, and also the most powerful and varied when it comes to scenic beauty. Troms has everything, from undulating farmland, to barren fishing stations; from chalk-white beaches, to alpine peaks. Troms is Norway in miniature. In just a day, the coastal steamer can traverse this "mini-Norway".

In the midst of this land of adventure lies the city of Tromsø, situated on the island that has given it its name. No other city in Norway has such fantastic natural beauty at its doorstep. On the mainland, just across the narrow sound, a

1200-metre-high pinnacle shoots straight up into the air. And only a two-hour brisk walk from Storgata, the city's main street, will find you at its summit. A fifteen-minute car ride, and you can strap on your skis and set off into one of the most wonderful mountain areas on Kvaløy, the island west of Tromsø. Only a ten-minute walk from the center of town lies the lighted ski run, where Tromsø residents entertain themselves cross-country skiing late into winter evenings.

In Tromsø, the ski season lasts until June, when you can ski in shorts and shirtless, or wearing a bikini, at a thousand metres, then schuss down to green lawns, and birches in fresh bloom. In this land of contrasts, it is both summer and winter at the same time.

While the ship takes a few hours of well-deserved rest at the dock in Tromsø, you can sample the city's scenic delights by taking the city's gondola up to Fløya. There you will find both a restaurant, and a view that will take the breath away of even the most jaded of tourists.

Two-hundred-year-old Tromsø was founded on trade, shipping, the export of fish, and hunting in the polar regions.

All Aboard!

■

May voyage is like sailing through three seasons. You may depart from a summer-warm Bergen, hit the green of springtime a couple of days further north, and end up in the white of winter north of Tromsø – like here passing the Lyngen peninsula.

The opening of a major bridge in 1962 marked the advent of modern times for Tromsø. The first in a series of bridges to be built in northern Norway, it became a model for all the others. And the fact that it connected Tromsø to the mainland made the city more attractive for investment.

Four years later came the airport, which lies on the west side of the island. Within ten minutes of landing, you can be strolling down Storgata. And the flight to Oslo takes two hours. Previously it took an entire day: first several hours by bus, and then by plane.

In 1972 the university arrived, – the third milestone in the city's recent history. It is situated on the northern part of the island, beside the brand new hospital – northern Norway's largest, and the country's most modern. Tromsø has become the city everyone flies into, a northern Norwegian capital with busy people coming and going from points north and south every day of the year.

At one time the city was just a little collection of wooden houses on the hillside down by the busy Tromsø channel. Now it has spilled out over its borders. On the mainland, just across from Tromsø proper, homes, townhouses, apartment complexes and bedroom communities extend for miles and miles. On the neighbouring island to the west, construction is expanding. There is certainly enough of this city to go around: Tromsø is Norway's largest municipality in terms of its physical size. With its 2500

The mightiest of them all, the Lyngsalpene "alps" in Troms. Seen here in April.

■

■

Modern technology and many years of experience join forces on the bridge. Even with state-of-the-art technology, a mate's good old-fashioned sea savvy will always be in demand.

Die Nordgehende verlässt Tromsö an einem Sommerabend. Im Hintergrund die Eismeerkathedrale am Fuß des Berges Tromsdalstind, ganzjährig ein beliebtes Ausflugsziel der Tromsöer.

■

square kilometres, it is five times larger than Oslo.

It is still possible to hasten slowly to this city, to let the ship take care of your journey, and give your soul a flight of fancy. This is the major differ-ence – between travelling by plane and travelling on the coastal steamer.

This is the way we arrived in Tromsø one January day, having plied the waters north-ward in lee of the beautiful island of Senja, until the city came into view over the bow. It lay there like a sparkling pre-cious jewel against the dark heavens of the Arctic night.

ON TOP OF THE WORLD

Three hours north of Tromsø, the Lyngsalpene (the Lyng Alps) sail up to us on the starboard side. This is northern Norway's most rugged mountain area. With peaks up to 1800 metres high, it is an eldorado for hardy types who can withstand mountain temperatures, and one of the most sought-after mountain climbing areas in Europe. Just after this, the port of Skjervøy pops up, sheltered on a hillside running up to a jagged peak that has snow in its crevices even in midsummer.

After Skjervøy, we head out to the Lopphavet sea, the fifth and second to last of the areas of open sea on the journey north. The border to Finnmark, Norway's northernmost county, crosses right in the middle of this sea. The people of this county have more room to play

■

Skjervøy is the last port of call before Finnmark, Norway's nothernmost and most sparsely populated county. Though it is only late July, winter is not far away.

than anywhere else in the country, with 0,6 square kilometres per resident. It will take 72 hours for the ship to sail around this northernmost county and return to Lopphavet again.

You will notice a big change when you leave the county of Troms and enter Finnmark. It is as if the beauty is cut off at Skjervøy, according to a captain I know. A pilot friend of mine put it this way: I like being in Finnmark best – the mountain plains, the vastness; here there

is space, and room, and air to breathe. These are the makings of a fantastic experience.

Regardless of how you feel about Finnmark, the first call in Finnmark makes an impression on an outsider. A few hours earlier he has been introduced to Skjervøy, nestled into hillside above the harbour, surrounded by green fields and snowy alpine peaks. Then he meets Øksfjord, a cluster of houses clinging to the foot of a pile of stones – a rock slide just waiting to happen. For above their living-room windows there is a several-hundred-metre-high slope littered with boulders.

Remove just one little chip of a stone at the foot of this stony slope, and Øksfjord would tumble down and be swept into the sea in the blink of an eye. With binoculars, wires and bolts can be seen. A resident of Øksfjord's life hangs by a slender thread. His consolation: these threads are made of steel.

The coastal steamer takes on a new role along the coast of Finnmark. You notice this at the ports of call. There are more people on the docks than there were farther south. There is a greater sense of expectation in the air, and the arrival of the coastal steamer means something even for those who are not travelling, or even expecting a package. For the inhabitants, a trip to the dock is a fleeting foray out into the big world.

The cargo also tells its story. Milk, bread, butter and meat are hoisted over the railing – everyday supplies that will find their way into each and every kitchen. And not to be forgot-

■

A coastal steamer at the dock in Skjervøy one night during the Easter holiday. Soon she will cast off and sail through the glitter of moonlight. Photo: Dag Nævestad.

■

Sailing in good weather in Øksfjord, with Norway's fifth largest glacier, Øksfjordjøkelen, 1166 meters above sea level, to starboard.

ten, the ship brings "the fruits of the south": carrots, potatoes, and cabbage. The repercussions of bad weather forcing the coastal steamer to pass by, or an engine problem that takes her off the route, can be felt in every home.

From Lopphavet to Honningsvåg, the ship sails mostly in protected waters. But from then on, as we travel eastward,

this protective bulwark of skerries disappears. Now there is nothing but the steep, barren mountainscape to fasten your eyes upon, rugged and black, rising vertically from the sea. But here and there in this inhospitable wasteland, an arm of a fjord, or a bay opens up, and the ship nips in.

First comes Kjøllefjord; just on the other side of the bird

refuge, Sværholtklubben. Then we sail around Nordkyn to Mehamn. From now on the ship is at the mercy of the Barents Sea, and we head southeast. After Mehamn, we pass Gamvik. It is no longer a port of call, and thus can only watch the northbound ship head out over Tana fjord, setting course for Berlevåg and Båtsfjord. Toward morning the ship sails into the

The same question as always:
Will we see the midnight sun?
On this particular May night the sun
broke through the clouds while the
ship was quayside in Berlevåg,
bathing the fishing boat and
landscape in a red glow.
Minutes later it had hidden its
glory behind the clouds again.

harbour at Vardø. By then 12 hours have passed since she set out from Honningsvåg. Four large lighthouses have guided her through: Slettnes, Kjølnes, Makkaur and Vardø.

The rest of our journey is a piece of cake. We sail in Varangerfjord to Vadsø, then on to our final stop, Kirkenes. The coastal steamer has sailed around what is referred to as the northern "scull cap". Kirkenes is at the same latitude as Tromsø – and almost as far east as the border with Russia.

In Finnmark's coastal areas, summer comes in fits and starts. A couple of nice warm days and then the fog rolls in from the sea, hangs cold and gray over headlands and fishing settlements, chasing people into their homes, while the mercury drops toward zero. The natives freeze for a day or two, and then comfort themselves with an old friend – indefatigable hope. They think – as fishermen are wont to do – that there will be better days, and anticipate that an easterly wind from Russia will clear the way for a continuation of summer. It has happened that they have hoped in vain, and then the standard explanation is: Summer was on a Friday this year.

My first meeting with Finnmark was more than forty years ago, at the end of June. I had been curious about my own country, and had taken a summer job on the coastal steamer. In spite of the season, I had expected arctic air. But the farther north we travelled, the more summer weather we had. We rounded the North Cape on a mirror-like sea in temperatures rivalling those of Miami Beach.

At the dock in Honningsvåg there was not even a hint of a breeze, and it was a relief to go down in the hold and load cargo. On the bridge, the thermometer read 30 degrees centigrade. Forward in the bow, the girls of the crew were laid out one after the other in the sun. They had spread blankets between the windlass, the post and the ropes and rigged up their own promenade deck. Pale, white bodies in bras and panties greedily soaked up the sun without a thought of their upcoming sunburn.

Summer or winter, north of the Arctic Circle it's always a good idea to bring a good warm cap along with you!

■

The passengers sat dazed with disbelief in their deck chairs as we cast off and sailed east toward Kjøllefjord. They found it hard to believe that it was the Arctic Ocean they were cutting a wake through.

I had the vent hole in my cabin open before I went on watch. A mild tradewind caressed my face, and reflected on

Right: What is left of a fishing smack built in 1912. A winter stroll along the shore while the ship is at the quayside may teach you about the past as well as the present of life in the far north.

■

■

The southbound ship docks in Hammerfest in the middle of a busy morning. If you're feeling energetic, a brisk walk up the hill is rewarded with a splendid view of the town and the islands around. Here, in the world's most northerly city, the sun never sets from May 17th to July 28th. But the winter night lasts from November 21st to January 23rd.

Europe's northernmost pinnacle rises to a majestic 307 metres over the Arctic Sea, and has served as a landmark for navigators since the days of yore. The first tourists arrived in the 1600's, but it wasn't until a king – the Swedish-Norwegian King Oscar II – paid a visit in 1873, that tourism took off.

■

my door was a golden ball of light that rose and fell. Up and down, up and down in long lazy swells. It was the sun shining through the vent hole, straight from the north.

We called at Vardø at midnight, and you would think they were expecting the king. Young and old alike, mothers with baby carriages, entire families, arrived in great numbers. Most of them were not expecting anyone, neither were they going to travel on the ship. They simply couldn't afford to sleep away the summer nights.

Twelve hours later, we were

back in Vardø, now southbound. The old, deserted dock was covered in a blanket of fog, and a measly five to six degrees centigrades was all the thermometer had to show for itself.

I was on watch in the bow as we sailed west from Vardø.

Bundled up in the ship's special Finnmark's coat, an old foul-smelling ankle-length coat with sheepskin lining that was flecked with pitch. I stood with my chin on the forward railing, as far forward as you can get without actually being out in the sea.

Gusts of icy wind tear at my cheeks and the corners of my eyes, I stare into the fog, and all I see is grey, grey, and more grey. Behind me I hear the playful mast trying to spook me. We've lost the bridge. It is as if the back half of the ship has been sawed off.

MIS "Richard With" dominates the harbour at the fishing station of Vardø in East Finnmark. For the resident population, the coastal steamer is still the vital nerve for their existence. But Vardø is vulnerable to rough weather conditions, and at times the ship has no choice but to sail past the harbour with its passengers and freight.

■

Every spring the Sami nomads trek out to the coast with their flocks of reindeer. Some of them have branched out into tourism. On your way to the North Cape you can buy Sami handcraft – perhaps from this rather splendid businessman!

The foghorn keeps me company, entertaining me with the long, deep modulated voice of a bassoon. Then from somewhere farther out, I hear a report from a proper and serious tuba. Off the port side a tempera-mental alto horn pipes up. The sea washes along the side of the vessel. I feel like the only stringed instrument – one who happens to have a cold – as I stand there holding watch in the midst of this orchestra.

We sail on like this for awhile in a groundswell of goodwill. Then, in one fell swoop, the blanket of fog lifts.

There is a patch of sky, and then a space opens up. We are sailing in a cathedral with blue awnings, and a marble floor.

Then one of the walls of fog tumbles down, and the Arctic Sea opens up before us. The concert subsides. To starboard is an overloaded Russian vessel weaving its way toward Archangel. Then another wall crumbles and slowly the marble floor expands. A rusted trawler, tight on our port side, follows the same course as we follow.

Behind us lies the land, a gray-black strip between the sea and the light cloud cover, like a huge flat slab of rock thrust up from the sea.

I let my eyes take in the scenario. The sun warms my face and I totally forget that my mission is over. I snap to at the sound of a voice over the loudspeaker, unmistakably that of our captain: Have you fallen asleep, deck hand, or have you become a tourist?

Eleven of the coastal steamers' ports of call are in Finnmark. This tells you something about the size and extent of this county, and what the daily calls of the coastal steamer mean to the people of Norway's northernmost county.

A fisherman once put it this way: "We are onboard our fishing boats, watching different types of ships sail by. They don't concern us. But then the coastal steamer comes along, and the guys straighten themselves. This is our boat! It forms a bond among all of us along the coast. But time and tides will take their toll on the coastal steamer, and the ships will find their way to the scrapyard and be made into nails. I

would really like to own one of those nails! By Jove! – I'd use it as a tie-clip!"

Even though it is the fisheries that maintain the livelihood of the majority of the eleven calls along the coast of Finnmark, each port has its own unique personality. Honningsvåg is the busy tourist center, and gateway to the North Cape. Twenty-four hours a day in the tourist season it buzzes with the sound of foreign tongues. But the snow-breaks up on the hillside, and the fishing boats shooting in and out of the busy harbour, remind us of everyday life and its challenges; of a life of battling the elements.

Kirkenes – the last stop, and the turning point of the voyage – lying at the innermost point of a sheltered arm of a fjord, has en entirely different story to tell. The history of Kirkenes is the history of Norway's largest mining community. Since the turn of the century, iron ore has been excavated by a gigantic mining operation near the Russian border. Slag heaps as high as mountains loom in the landscape just outside the city, which is becoming less and less of a mining town with each year that passes. Now Kirkenes is setting its sights on becoming the headquarters for activity in the Barents Sea.

During the war, Kirkenes was one large German fortress, "Festung Kirkenes". Up to 100,000 German soldiers were stationed here, and the city was the air base for attacks on allied convoys in the north. There is a monument to "The Red Army Soldier" in the center of town as a reminder of the city's dra-

matic history as a base of attack for Hitler's failed advance on Murmansk. Kirkenes was liberated from the east, by Russian troops.

Vadsø, on the other side of Varangerfjord, is the county seat. It is a city whose character reflects the effects of immigration from Finland. It lies at the foot of an impressive plateau, and in the winter, it is an eldorado for cross-country skiing.

Vardø, a few hours farther out in the fjord, is a different story. A rain-drenched, weather-beaten fishing community, at one time it was Norway's largest fishing settlement and did extensive trade with its Russian neighbours in the east. A few years ago there was a "plant a tree" campaign in Finnmark. Sharp tongues would have it that Vardø didn't want to participate – because they "already had a tree".

Actually, Vardø has one tree – and that's it. In return they take good care of it, covering it in winter so it will survive until each new spring arrives. You will find *the* tree at the city's impressive fortress, dating from the fourteenth century.

Of the ports of call along the coast of Finnmark, Berlevåg has, perhaps, the most distinctive history. It is the history of the battle of man against the sea. In 1882, a large storm swept over the city, grounding a large part of the fishing fleet. A quarter of a century later, the Arctic Sea again cast itself upon this little fishing community leaving its harbour area wasted.

At this time, the fishermen sent a resolution to Parliament demanding that Berlevåg be

Much more fun on the coastal steamer! Three teenagers on their way south at the close of the school year in Finnmark. When you travel by boat, you travel at such a rate that you and your soul travel together, arriving at your destination at the same time!

■

The farther north you are, the more important the coastal steamer. In the fishing settlement of Kjøllefjord, the steamers bring margarine to the breakfast table, engine parts to the fishing boat – and the latest fashions from mail-order houses down south.

given a proper harbour. The Ports' authorities arrived and started to build jetties. Several twenty-tonblocks of rock were dynamited out of the mountainside and freighted out into the harbour on a specially build railway – the world's northernmost. The work took time, as construction could only take place in the summer months, and not always then.

Twice within a period of 25 years storms destroyed what the port authorities had built up. The blocks of stone were no match for the Arctic Sea. The last time the sea attacked was in January, 1959, when 90 metres of the western arm of the jetty went down, and three seasons of hard work were lost.

A French invention called a "tetrapode", a four-armed cement device that compresses and become stronger the more the sea attacks it, provided a solution. It took three generations to secure the harbour at Berlevåg. In 1976, both of the jetties were completed, and they have held ever since. But just in case, at the western jetty, there is a stock of tetrapodes in the event that the impossible should occur.

There are two monuments in Berlevåg. One honours those who fell in battle; the other is a tetrapode on a pedestal. This French-patented cement construction has become the symbol of the people of Berlevåg's victory over the sea.

Although this industrious fishing community had finally managed to build a protected harbour for its fishing fleet, it still needed a dock at which to receive coastal steamers. A forty-foot open shuttle was the residents' only connection to the rest of the world. The coastal steamer would anchor

If you're lucky you may get invited up to the bridge. It looks like the cockpit of a DC9, and is pretty well incomprehensible for ordinary mortals. But with the right person as your guide, it can be an unforgettable experience.

■

As far north as you can get on the European continent. Nordkyn, a jagged pinnacle, at 71 degrees, 8 minutes north, soars upward from the sea. Beyond, wait Berlevåg, Båtsfjord, Vardø.

out in the harbour. The shuttle would pull along-side, and passengers would climb up and down a ladder placed along the side of the ship.

In stormy weather, the shuttle would bob up and down along the side of the ship like a piece of cork. When this happened, the passengers had to go onboard just like cargo: through the air in a basket. When this happened to you, there was but one thing left to do: put your faith in the Lord – and the seaman manning the winch.

In 1974, Berlevåg got its dock. The residents have since pulled the trusty 40-foot shuttle ashore, built a structure around it, and made it into a museum.

"Do people live here all year round?" It happened that I was asked such questions from foreign tourists when I worked as a travel guide on the coastal steamer. Without exception, the question was first posed when we had come as far north as Finnmark.

I must admit that on my first trip around the "scull" as a young deck hand, I found myself asking the same question. Was such a barren, rocky, and windswept coast so far to the north inhabitable?

Then I started going ashore. My first meeting with the outpost of Berlevåg still lives vividly in my memory. I had met a native of Berlevåg on a dock further south. We had started up a conversation – such things happen easily in the north. I once read an interview with an Italian who had travelled extensively in Norway. "Indeed", he said, "the farther north I come

in Norway, the farther south I feel have come in Italy!"

We had started talking to each other, and the man from Berlevåg invited me home with him on the spot. The northbound ship stood at the dock ready to hoist anchor. My new acquaintance was about to go onboard, I had only to purchase a ticket and follow him. The time between the first and third calls of the departure bell was all it took for us to get to know each other and for me to buy my ticket.

In the course of a few days as a guest in his house, I had to abandon my misconceptions. My host figuratively grabbed me by the nape of the neck and marched me out upon soft, mossy plateaus covered with flowers; showed me fertile green valleys with birch wood, and cabin life, and babbling brooks. All of this and more lie right outside this man's door. Proudly, he had shared with me his countryside, and his roots.

He was no less enthusiastic when he described winter skies aflame with the northern lights, ski trips over the mountain plains at Easter, and autumn evenings, when the electricity is down, and the house is being shaken up by a storm. "But we ride it out!", he says of the storm.

On the way home again on the coastal steamer I got into a conversation with a woman from the fishing settlement of Mehamn, farther to the west, from whom I also learned an essential lesson. "I don't think you people in the south really understand these small communities. Even though there is

Berlevåg's history is the history of man's battle against the sea. It took three generations before this community was able to build a jetty capable of resisting the might of the Arctic Sea.

■

"Good old Guttormsen" – a legend among captains and officers. For 40 years he served the coastal steamers – the first 20 without a dock. He had Norway's most unique job description: shuttle driver! He carried passengers and cargo to and from the ships on an open shuttle, in all types of weather, all year round. In 1974, Berlevåg got its coastal steamer dock, and the shuttle has been pulled ashore and made into a museum.

■

often no place as cold or barren, warmth and contentment can always be found behind the grey rocks. This is the stuff that moulds people, and this is why we hold these places of ours so dear. There are indeed no roots that cling so tightly as those that grow near a stone. They endure!"

Many years later, I went ashore in Finnmark, this time to live there, and had the chance to really experience winter along the Arctic Sea. I recall one December voyage on the "Harald Jarl" eastbound for Kirkenes, where I was living with my family.

I pack myself in layers of warm clothing and go on deck. I want to take in the view of the wide sound up toward Honningsvåg on my morning stroll. I choose my course, deciding to go from the bridge, down the stairs to the boat deck, round to the stern and up to the bridge again. Round and round I go, stopping now and then in front of the open door to the engine room, turning my back to the crosscurrent of diesel fumes that stream up from the ship's interior.

Eventually the warmth of the engine room is forgotten, and my rounds become fewer. We are in a mystical land, sailing on a deep-blue sea surrounded by glowing white marble. Down to the south a strip of sky blushes, sending its pale violet-red aura northward – a promise that the sun will return some time in January.

But it is on the opposite side of the ship that I find myself riveted to the railing. Before me is a cornflower blue sky positioned like a dome over the silhouette of a shining marble island. The blue-black sea in the foreground is a dramatic contrast to the white backdrop.

Then we travel in open sea for a stretch, the deck undulating gently. Somewhere off in the distance lies the North

Northbound along the
Finnmark coast in March.
Havøysund next.
Many tourists prefer the winter
sailings. They are cheaper and less
crowded. And the snow-covered
landscape takes on an even more
fairyland appeal. It's just a matter
of being adventurous. But don't
forget your warm
winter woolies!

■

The coastal steamer has been to
Kirkenes, and is on its way back.
In the course of the day, a strip of
land with a cluster of houses on it
will appear on the horizon.
This is Vardø, Norway's
easternmost city. It is an island
community, dependent on
the fish in the sea and
at the mercy of the
weather gods.

Cape, deserted – abandoned for the winter.

But what is happening along the ridge of the island aft and to the port side? A reddish gold hump rises slowly. A little further up the sound, the hump has become an impressive full moon, rolling like a wheel along the snow-covered ridge. It is as if it is a cardboard cut-out, and we are sailing along in a landscape of theatre props.

I stand there mesmerised – and frozen to the bone. I have extra clothes in my cabin, but don't want to take the time to fetch them. We are on our way up Magerøysundet sound now. This means narrower sea lanes; the mountains move in closer. We ascend this blue-black sea, which sometimes glows with phosphor. A pale rose colour

"Quer durch den Roten Kontinent" ... Through the red continent. A German passenger on her way to the North Cape relaxes on deck with a book about the intense heat of Australia, well on the way to the opposite end of the world!

lies upon the white mountain-sides. It is as if the light has been filtered, as the skies to the south cast their frugal aura.

There is a gentle arc in among all the sharp lines. A piece of flatland, a house, smoke from a chimney.

There is a gentler scene in among all the sharp lines. A stretch of flat land, a house, smoke from a chimney, and a light in a window. Here, where land and sea meet, is a typical Finnmark dwelling, frozen in wintry hibernation.

■

The coast of Finnmark is harsh but fascinating. Sailing up through Magerøysund towards Honningsvåg.

HOLIDAYS AND CELEBRATIONS ON BOARD

Women give birth onboard; and people die. Birthdays – especially 50th 60th, and 70th birthdays – are celebrated, and if you're lucky, you will find yourself in the middle of a wedding under sail, or have a "bride" celebrating her silver wedding anniversary at your table at dinner. An altar is part of the inventory on the newest ships. The coastal steamer is familiar with all aspects of humanity.

Although the coastal steamer is considered the workhorse of the coast, she does not let any of the holidays slip by unnoticed. Many spend their Easter holiday onboard, thus sailing through two season – beginning with the green of springtime in the south and sailing into the white of winter in the north. If Easter comes late in the year, the days in northern Norway will be even longer than the days in the south. You can sit on the deck and sun yourself, while watching a Norway that is still dressed for winter glide by.

Especially popular are the Christmas voyages. There is a special mood – a special sense of expectation – onboard. The chef prepares authentic Norwegian Christmas dishes and in such abundance that you feel like you are going to burst. The Christmas tree is decorated and in place, secured to both floor and ceiling. Santa, a mate or radio operator disguised for the occasion, comes tramping in with his sack full of surprises. When church bells all over the land announce the coming of Yuletide, the ship hastens to the nearest harbour, where it is met by both the choir and the vicar. Passengers and crew alike gather together in the saloon to celebrate. A few extra hours on shore, then the captain stands on the bridge: Hoist anchor! he commands, and we sail into the Yuletide night.

So popular are these Christmas Eve celebrations at sea that many residents of the coast buy a ticket and go onboard, joining the voyage for a day or two to experience the Express Route's spirit and warmth, and to enjoy the chef's Christmas buffet. I had long dreamed of celebrating Christmas on the coastal steamer. I embarked one Christmas eve, early in the day, in Kirkenes. It was a day and a night I will always remember. The approach to the holiday stillness of Vadsø at the lightest hour of the day, past a jetty covered with a frosty icing and shining magically in the blue-gray half-light. Fishing vessels tethered to their buoys, their rigging covered with rime, rolling languidly in the waves from the ship.

Vardø, a few hours later: a boy with a sled, a taxi with its "vacant" sign lit atop of it, the red postal truck, and a warmly-clad dock hand; this was the entire welcoming committee. Leaving the ship, a grandfather balances himself as he walks along the landing carrying a tricycle wrapped in Christmas paper; a young girl on her way home to her family stumbles along in her high-heels. Two passengers and an almost empty sack of delayed Christmas mail, and that was it for Vardø. The mate swings the gate shut and the ship pokes its nose out into the Arctic Sea.

Apparently, the sea has also taken a holiday. We cut a wake through lazy swells and head northwest toward Båtsfjord. By five o'clock we're parallel to the Makkaur lighthouse. I stand on the deck in my duffel-coat, resting my elbows on the icy

teak railing. Summer deck chairs are bound up in groups and stacked in a corner. Astern, the deck is covered with an inch of snow, without a track in it.

The vessel lists. We have rounded the cape and bear in toward the mouth of Båtsfjord fjord. A bit further, we see the tip of a strip of light. This is from the houses at the furthest reach of a fishing settlement. As soon as we are securely moored, the gong sounds. Streaming into the dining-room, in their best clothes, are chambermaids, deck hands, the radio operator and the machin-ist – and the skipper himself. He goes from table to table, shaking hands and wishing a Merry Christmas to one and all, before we all move into the lounge for cake and coffee, and

■

Christmas on board the coastal steamer is unlike any other Christmas, with the warm atmos-phere in the decorated saloons, and the fascinating winter light outside. To the north the flames of the Northern Lights; to the south the glow of the winter sun. At Christmas time a special calm descends upon the ship, though that doesn't stop Santa Claus paying a visit! Perhaps you might be out on deck in the falling snow of deep midwinter as the captain guides his ship trough the Christmas night.

presents from the Seamen's Mission.

And, while the southbound ship rolls along toward Berle-våg, we bravely balance oursel-ves in a dance around the Christmas tree, seeking support by joining hands, united in spite of that fact that we sing of the Child born in Bethlehem in several different tongues.

Go onboard again five months later, in the middle of May, and you will find that you have lan-ded right in the middle of the colourful celebration of Nor-way's national day. May 17th, always referred to as "The Seventeenth of May", is the other time of the year when

everything in Norway stops. On this day Norwegians celebrate the signing of their Constitution, dating from 1814. There are no military parades – this day belongs to the children, and to the thousands of children's parades held all over Norway.

I once boarded a southbound ship in Bodø the night before May 17th. A few hours later, I jumped out of my bunk. Had I been dreaming, or were we being fired upon? I ran up on deck only to find that we were moored in the idyllic town of Ørnes. It was only 7 o'clock in the morning, and yet up on the ridge behind the houses, gunpowder filled the air. Ørnes had launched the big day with a thundering salute.

Even the most hard of hearing residents must have surely been awakened.

In Nesna, farther south, the coastal steamer is a part of the celebration. The captain scruti-

■

At many of the ports of call the coastal steamer is a regular feature in the celebrations on 17th May – Norway's national day. At Nesna (top, opposite page) children wait while the southbound ship docks, and captain and passengers join the procession up to the town square. In Harstad, passengers wake to the rousing music of marching bands. But on board ship too the day is celebrated, as seen here with the ship rounding West Finnmark on its way from Hammerfest to Havøysund.

nises our speed – we must be on time. We list to one side as the "Kong Olav" sails into the dock. The head of the children's parade is just visible behind the buildings on the pier. The children stand impatiently, wearing their party shoes and stamping their feet on the wet concrete. The police chief, spiffed-up-for-the-occasion, stands at the head of the parade, followed by flag-bearers, the parade committee, a brass band, and the children of the town en masse.

The gangplank is put in place and the starting gun is fired. Then the residents of Nesna march along the side of the ship, singing and cheering, and screaming their heads off. Those onboard, both crew and passengers, look down over the

landing , and then are swept along in the colourful parade, eventually finding themselves in the town square in time for the main speech of the day.

A half hour later, we are underway again. But suddenly we reduce our speed, turn, and return to the dock. What now?

Two shame-faced German tourists stand on the dock. They got carried away with their picture-taking, and forgot all about ships and departure times. Nor could they know that they have not yet seen their last parade today.

The captain stands ready

with his flag, and we gather on the boat deck for our own Seventeenth of May parade! Onboard the "Kong Olav", a merry and flag-bedecked party of fellow travellers march round and round the afterdeck, while the islets and skerries of northern Norway pass by the ship in their budding spring attire. The "King Olav" heads onward toward Sandnessjøen.

■

After the 17th May procession the captain treats passengers to champagne in the panorama saloon. In the evening there is high dinner in the restaurant, where everybody is given a national day ribbon.

A DIFFERENT KIND OF JOURNEY

The coastal steamer has celebrated its hundredth birthday. Storms have swirled around it – not just at sea, but also on land. There are politicians who maintain that subsidies to Norway's famous coastal route are too much of a drain on the economy. Many a Norwegian Minister of Transport and Communication has tried to cut costs, but without much success. Ministers come and ministers go – but that can also be said of the coastal steamer.

Once in the 1970's, a meddlesome Minister of Transport and Communication wanted to make Trondheim – or even Bodø, which is even farther north, the southernmost turning point of the voyage. This proposition was met with a wave of protest from one end of the country to the other. "We must not divide Norway in the middle!" thundered the head of the Finnmark county board.

The last time such a storm raged was in 1990. A dangerously high number of members of Parliament thought NOK 208 million annually was too much in subsidies for a route that was being used more and more by foreign tourists. When Parliament gathered to debate the issue, it was the coastal steamer's right "to be, or not to be" that was in question.

Whether anyone had realized it before or not, it soon

The "Narvik" belongs to the second youngest generation of coastal steamers, along with the "Vesterålen" and the "Midnatsol" – all of which were built in Norway in the early 1980's. Here the "Narvik" sails into Havøysund on a summer morning.

became clear that the coastal steamer continued to be an object of national pride, dear to the hearts of Norwegians – a unique institution whose worth could not be measured in terms of money. The existence of the coastal steamer is an issue larger than the politics of transportation. It is a national symbol. Representatives from north and south, and east and west, stood up and demanded emphatically: LET THE COASTAL STEAM ER LIVE!

On the third day of debate, the supporters of the coastal steamer's proposal was pushed through by two votes. With

this, the foundation was laid for a powerful new initiative. With the smallest majority possible, Parliament accepted the ship-owners' desire for an eleven year period of transition, and NOK 1,875 billion in support for the running and revitalisation of the fleet. The ship-owners for their part, pledged to invest NOK 1.3 billion.

∎

In the panorama saloon you can always enjoy the scenery – whatever the weather outside.

From the year 2002, the coastal steamer should sail under its own steam, without support from the state.

The vital nerve, vital artery, the backbone of the coast – these are over-used words, but they still have validity. For parts of the coastal population, the coastal steamer is still "Coastal Highway Number 1". From the very beginning, in 1893, tourists have found their way to the coastal steamer. Its ships made Norway world famous as "The Land of the Midnight Sun". For a long time the majority of the foreigners onboard were

■

*Waiting for the first course...
The sea air whets the appetite.
The restaurant staff are part of
the ship's soul. In the summer season
many of them are language students.
(Photo: Knut Hjelvik)*

*At most of the ship's ports of call the
costal steamer stops long enough for
you to go ashore and observe the
character of the place. Like here in the
main street in Tromsø, with houses
dating back to before 1900.
In late April.*

■

British. In later years, there has been a greater showing from the continent, and today Germans dominate the passenger list for most sailings.

You don't need to be a foreigner to think it is quite an experience to see Norway from the deck of a coastal steamer. Even seamen onboard, with ten and twenty years service, catch themselves standing alongside

*No matter how cold
and wintery it is in the
main street in Tromsø –
a pint of the local brew
warms the
cockles of the heart. But
it's got to be a pint of
Mackøl – the pride of
the Arctic city.*

■

the tourists at the railing – just to look, even though they have seen it all many times before.

What – in addition to the scenic beauty – can it be that makes the coastal steamer so sought after that there is a battle for accommodation in the high season?

It cannot possibly be the exotic night-life onboard, because there is none. Neither are there cabarets or casinos. Of course, a local passenger may bring out his harmonica and get everybody in the mood for a dance on deck. You cannot even find a duty-free bar on-board. The coastal steamer plies waters close to the rocky coast-lines – well inside the strict Norwegian customs borders.

Is it the climate perhaps? No, not that either. On the coastal steamer you have to be prepared for snow flurries even in June, and always have a warm cap and a scarf in your suitcase.

What is it that causes tour-ists from all over the world to fight for a booking on this coastal route, instead of cruis-ing along the coast on a luxury liner?

The answer is: they come

because it is different; because it is an everyday route, and not just for tourists. Because it offers more than just the sea voyage and the scenery that the luxury cruise ships offer. The trip is always more than just visually pretty; it is interesting, it is educational, and it is exciting.

"The world's most beautiful voyage", according to the travel brochures. Captains, tour guides, and shipping companies can attest to a stream of accolades. Even the most well-travelled foreigners who have seen most of what there is to see in the world, speak with reverence of the coastal steamer. They've never experienced anything like it!

■

And perhaps this will be your favourite memory from your voyage on a Norwegian costal steamer – that fabulous night at the top of the world when you completely forgot to go to bed!

All good things must come to an end – even a voyage on the coastal steamer. But it is always possible to set sail again. There are those who do so over and over again, knowing that one's twentieth voyage is "on the house".

∎

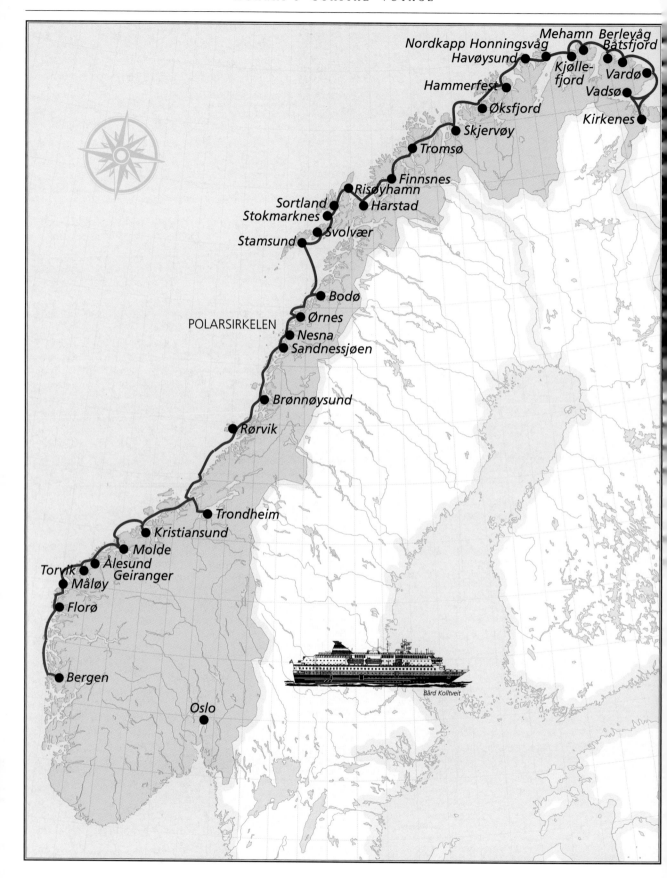

Nordkapp Honningsvåg
Mehamn Berlevåg
Båtsfjord
Havøysund
Hammerfest
Kjølle-
fjord
Øksfjord
Vardø
Vadsø
Skjervøy
Kirkenes
Tromsø
Finnsnes
Risøyhamn
Sortland
Harstad
Stokmarknes
Svolvær
Stamsund
Bodø
Ørnes
POLARSIRKELEN
Nesna
Sandnessjøen
Brønnøysund
Rørvik
Trondheim
Kristiansund
Molde
Torvik
Ålesund
Måløy
Geiranger
Florø
Bergen
Oslo

Bård Kolltveit